ETERNITY OF

Domonique Young

Publisher's Cataloging-in-Publication Data

Provided by Five Rainbows Cataloging Services

Names: Young, Domonique, author.

Title: Eternity of Dreams / Domonique Young.

Description: Carson, CA: Domonique Young, 2020.

Identifiers: ISBN 978-1-7379128-1-1

Subjects: LCSH: Poetry. | Autobiographical poetry. | Grief. | Love.
| Single mothers. | BISAC: POETRY / Subjects & Themes / Death,
Grief, Loss. | POETRY / Women Authors.

Classification: LCC PS3625.O46 E84 2020 (print) | LCC
PS3625.O46 (ebook) | DDC 811/.6--dc23.

Author: Domonique Young

Cover Photograph: Domonique Young

ACKNOWLEDGMENT

I would like to thank the Lord for the talent He gave me to bless the world. I'm forever grateful to Him. I would love to dedicate this book to my three amazing children, who made everything worthwhile. I wouldn't want to change for anything. I'm blessed to be their mom. I'll always love you. My Grandma, who became an angel in 2001, thanks for loving me and being a Mother to me that I couldn't even dream would be possible. When my mother passed, that was the day that my heart beat differently. The woman of my soul was no longer with me, but every morning the sun would shine for me. I know it was you mom. I was broken and lost. She never stopped fighting for me at all. I want to thank God for my birth mom, who gave me life and my grandma who was a mother to me. She keep me no matter what. Thank God for my father, who chose to give my mom the seed of life.

Thanks to everyone whom believed in me and the Eternity of Dreams poetry collection. I would like to thank the people who supported me in my life, who were there through my darkest moments, pushing me through the tunnel of light. I appreciate those who didn't believe in me at all. The negatives of so many people motivated me to grow. Thanks for thinking of me. Thanks for your thoughts. My Papa and Tia, my sisters, it has been so amazing to see you all grow. Thanks for loving me and my babies always invited us to family events. The years have been amazing what an honor to have you in our lives.

ETERNITY OF DREAMS
TABLE OF CONTENT

ENTERTAINMENT

Hi, it's me, the girl that you never paid any attention to. I was just there for entertainment purposes. There isn't a day that goes by without thinking of you; excuse me if I fell in love with you in deep thoughts, watching you sleep. When he wakes up the pleasure was all his; the way you play with my hair had me believing you cared for me. The

gate of my soul reopens the dance. I couldn't stop smiling. I was broken. He fixes me for a second. I went to sleep, and when I wake up, he was gone. When I was free, you had me role-playing in your show, how you were missing me. I have hung out with you long enough to see how you are, but this feeling between us could grow. Wishing I can go to an empty lot, I can visualize a whole Garden of lilies full of life; why does he read me like a book? You complete every area of me, but you don't want me. Then reality came in, and maybe I'm putting too much into it. Please excuse me. It's my emotion, the way you capture me. I haven't been able to be myself in a while. I just laugh, pure fun, with nothing else except the company of you. Please excuse me if I have found something new about you. I love your unknown path.

MY STORY

I love him so much, and nothing in the world matters except for him. I want to have a family with you and have a little piece that would be close to perfect. I want to melt in you as the sun disappears in the skies. My life was yours. My story has unfolded where there is a greater love besides myself. She has many hourglasses, sharp like broken glass. He's dancing to the music of my heart, he gets drunk with one taste, and the soul is mine. He is no longer the person. I love you before your habits start knocking on the door where friends know your favorite drink and keep you a while for entertainment, but to him, it's just having fun. The time spent can be spent with your kids. I never imagined being a single parent of two babies, but I walk by faith always. I have never changed my role as a mother for a man. My story is unfolding like water can't be held, so at the end of the day, it's just my two babies. He was in the world of having fun and dreams because reality is like a drug that gave you that high that you would never find again. I stayed in my position, and

never once was moved by your actions and my world still goes around my life, my story is my kids always & forever. I love you for giving me a piece of you where I can always remember that moment you were happy for your babies once upon a time before you disappeared in the cold hand of friends while your life becomes little to no value like paper money, look at you. The ride you're going down when you are gone, the only memory they will have about you, was a drunk, and your art talent, just wasted away nowhere to be found.

 *Domonique Young*

ITS HOPELESSNESS

I have given you the best of me, and in return, you gave me the worst of you. I am bewildered because I'm not in any category of this little girl who can't give you anything, just what is between her legs, the price of your health. You're so dark where the sun forgets your name and never shines for you. How can you wake up and go to sleep? Just pure disrespect. You look me in my eye, confident like it's normal to call me out by my name and accuse me of sleeping with your friends. They are like you. I guess you don't see the queen in me, lost in the street with these dogs with fleas, and it doesn't matter to you as long as you get a fix, sick twisted like a bad disease without the cure. You ask to lay with me, I laugh. Not even in your dreams, you can't taste me his dirty just like the girl who always is open 24 hours getting lunch money, thinking its life. He has made me into a beast where I ask a million questions before I give you help. I can't break my true self-worth. I'm still amazed after wasting time with the worst of you. I had to wake myself up and tell myself this can't be my

future husband or me. When you came around, dark clouds follow, and it's not worth my happiness at all. You never saw me as queen, never treated me like one. That is how you lost me forever, go and sleep with the dogs. He has giving himself away with no respect to self and your money because you never had self-love. Look at you; everything you touch is lifeless. The story of a queen who thought she could help you with your demons, its hopelessness.

BETTER DAYS

I had you in mind. Are we still living within the frame of our soul? I feel like we never left. How are you feeling? Your name is at the tip of my tongue, trying not to call him your name, and nothing could compare to you; please forgive me for the years of not being so caring to you. I had a part in it that bring my monster out. Why are you still present in my mind? From the moment my eyes open to the time they close, it's you. He gave me two beautiful children. All I ever wanted was a family I could have for myself and just be present for my children, but I know the journey will be with my children alone with a bag of hope left on a shelf; faith-building stairs as we go, no time for tears. I have to be strong for better days.

MARS

Oh Mars what a perfect smile you have. My soul was hot, my heart escaped for a moment, he gives me gifts and it fades away back to perfect. I was his favorite in a puppet show raining from an invisible cloud, it must be love, oh Mars what is this? It is new to me, the fun parts and the worst parts. It seems we always have strings tied to our souls with someone pulling them, it just happens in a moment I let go. I know it would be fun with you Mars, the obsession in me, I can see the craziness of your mind, my world became a maze for you where you can always find what the world was, and just as those tears would fall, your words would destroy my world like an ocean dancing through the city until there was nothing left except your shelter. I guess we're back to that sick side of you and it grows without light, not enough love, no communication and it grew from a made up love story where we draw the sun and call it perfect. Mars you were the best, I love you always, may the energy never detach us. Even though we are not together I can

feel you spiritually, just laughing without a plan, but thanks for the show made by Mars, you are truly a star and I am a shadow within your world following you, it's the closest to sit on the edge of the earth as your breath became like winter hands, your whole body filled with chills, what an amazing feeling to be loved in so many ways by just one person with multiple personalities.

February 15th, 2021

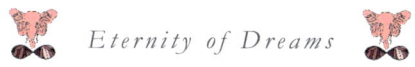

NO STORY LIKE MINE

I'm looking around, and I wonder why things have disappeared like time, I can't remember the second time to say hello. I'm running laps in my mind trying to figure out who I am. I am blessed to wake up each day. The best part of the days is when I am with my children, and it seems unreal that I am their mother. It is a blessing, my prince and princess. I cry like a raging ocean without direction, in and out of your soul. Pulled like strings my body is empty, and my heart hurts. The amazing feeling is to be one with a person and watch everything else fall together. I almost forget there is no story like mine...

I AM DIFFERENT

I'm a different story. You could not reach my level. I am untraceable, gifted, blessed and also wired by many. I have unlimited love, no matter if you have caused me pain. I'm in no one's catalog, and I don't need to fix myself for anyone to accept me, so you can get lost. I'm comfortable with myself. When night comes the dreams always welcome me, I am never judged. The arms of the skies that reach for me, the stars are always welcoming. I call it home.

STILL PHOTOS

The still photos of fake smiles captured for a moment until reality knocks on the door of your heart and it breaks into thousands of pieces. The photo still can't wipe all the tears you caused, the dreams without meaning, the answer why you can't be a man, how come your words don't dress me up as clothes. Give me the gratitude and blessing to be with you, but it's different; it seems the emotions you take always left me in the shadow of your madness. Where it became numb with no feeling of loving you, freeze in time in the midst of summer. I'm at a place where I will rather be a still photo than a present memory that you think you can control. I'll fly above space because I'm too valuable to be in your world. He can't see it. I'm not a subject; I'm the whole agenda plus more you couldn't even be on a level as me.

May 11, 2018

NEW DAY

When I see you, it is like the first time I met you; no matter how many years that have passed, I still love you growing like wild lily, getting better with the count of the stars suspended in space. What a dream to still be able to be in your eyes. When I see you time and time, it's not enough hours in a day. I'll always keep you day or night in my mind. I'm truly the image of your soul. It's a new day.

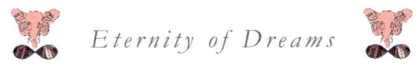

THE HAND OF TIMES

The hand of time carries your birthday, and it seems like a party that never ends. You're always absent from the party. I'm the only one lost in time where déjà vu comes knocking. Remember the day we created life entwined with no thought. I still love you even after the pain. I hear the clock ticking; do you hear it? Let us record history one more time, lost in our body like endless fields of lily smiling. I know what it brings, but I'll still bring you to life and give birth to an upcoming dream. The birth of our children reminds me of the time of the beginning of an amazing life. I couldn't wait to watch you and your sister grow. One day, time stopped for five months; my world was empty and quiet. I couldn't stop thinking of my dreams that I gave birth to the man who carried my soul, I loved him at his worst, and praised him at his best. Why would you invite the devil? He is sitting in jail like a foreign animal, 24 hours a day. She still wants to hold you through the night. She becomes still like water, and you don't hear the tick at all, just your soul

going to sleep. I record a message to say I love you always. I'll keep lighting the path for you I promise mommy will come back for you. I promise, just wait for the clock, it will remind you every minute, second, and also the hours how important you are to me; the faded memories of when we create dreams giving life, we love each other, but I know you never felt the same way I felt for you, the relationship of make-believe where everything seems real. The pain isn't real until you no longer are able to hide from reality; it came like an ocean washing over you, no more sandcastle, just time to remind us that we had two babies, we had set aside ourselves to give you the best of us, but you disappeared. It was only me carrying for this life, doing your part in your absence why you never came back for your dreams, but your soul is still dark when you go in a room no one notices you never shine. Everyone will see how dead your soul is; it is rotten inside out like a flower; it's a certain smell that catches your attention. The best of us records with the hands of this clock that reacts nonstop, it's my son's dream day then my daughter and then you. I'm here alone, still celebrating at the party that seems like it will never end, just waiting for something new to record. I love your time, the best of you; everything is still like the kiss of time freezing. The hand of time.

April 23

FALSE APPEARANCE

I'm a ghost working off the recording; just because you don't see me doesn't mean I don't have a master plan, laughing in the lab. She gets the right one when I appear. When your eyes meet mine, it's already done. I have already reached for your soul, drilled holes in your heart every time it beats a second off your life. I'm sitting here waiting and watching for your body to collapse like a building with a bomb in it. All the trouble you cause me, the hell you put my children through, hearing my daughter cry asking mom, when am I going home? You take the phone. I can't comfort her at all; it drives me wild. I remain calm, and I'm going to ride you like a horse to the bone. May God never bless you. I was a fool thinking you had me because you are my cousin. You caused me harm by keeping me from my babies; you are wicked. I was working in the lab, and your party is ending. My children will return home because there's nothing you can do to stop me at all. I'm a beast. You haven't heard it's me, the woman who gets released to her house untouched. I will

battle you for what's mine daily. I have no rest, and my soul is hungry. I love a challenge, a kiss from the morning. Let me know when it's time to reach your soul, watch your body fall again as you see me rise day by day. Thanks for your thoughts. I heard you are moving on. I felt empowered like I just wanted to be a ghost in your mind, pull your string as my name rolls off your tongue. I promise I'll never trust you again, the day my children return, you're dead to me. Well, every bad deed you wish for me, may you fall in the pool of your tears and drown in it as the breath escapes your lungs and is replaced with the same water. May I be the nightmare that keeps you company, and I will never let you kill me with a kiss of dark dreams that flow like a body of water. I'm still above everything untouched by your false appearance...

March 14

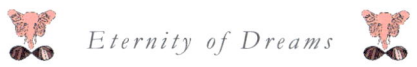

COLD TO THE TOUCH

The funniest thing is that you were never a father. What makes you a monster is that you put me in jail, separated me from my children, and I couldn't put a roof over their heads. You are sneaky like a snake. I heard you, and I'm ready for battle. My mind is set, and you could never reach me. I'm still here in court as you showed your face, feeling proud, looking at me over your mistake, and what you caused me in my life. You will cry forever, and no one will help. Your soul will be trapped like jail; you will never be free. May God never bless you to be a part of my children's lives as they get older. "Dad" will fade like a sunset when they see your true self. I will not lower myself to bash you in anyway; if my children think the world of you, so be it. When they get older, here goes your karma.

You are a lonely old man. I know I will not be there when you take your last breath. Think of me. I hate the very core of your being; I wish your mom would have overdosed with you in her womb, your father getting abused by a man repeatedly until

your stomach spills out of every hole you have. May your mind became glass and dance around your heart, excuse me of my time of betrayal which I carried two lives made sure they were always safe. I didn't know you could harm me. When time stops and dreams no longer sleep. I'll battle you for my children cold to the touch.

March 13

CLOWN IN YOU

You give your whole life for the street, betrayed government information to just end up in a wheelchair. You wear the shoe and hat, and you must be a clown. You don't get any benefit from it, just a permanent reminder that you fell into a trap that coats your life. Beside these walls, we are brainwashed, thinking we have enemies but who knows us better than our parents, an enemy within ourselves. The street is full of motherless/fatherless children crying upon the earth, riding the hope of Mother Nature, no one doesn't tell me. My voice is like thunder looking for my child, knowing that the shadow got them, but they're not God, so they can't reach your soul. Angel wings, you're the prettiest thing I have ever seen, when is it going to end? I know if you touch mine, I'll uproot your whole family, and make sure you will never be able to produce anything. I'll close the door, will not open at all; that's just me, the mind of madness, and hopeless people. The people send you out to the army to fight other countries that are blind to the range of us. When we

are the problem, they blame others for a mistake they made and tell us to fight; made up wars when we are the enemy of the house controlled by a promise. We will take care of you. They came back with no memories, amputees, homeless, and made up enemies: hidden, motive unclear, ideal. You don't have the balls to fix your issues, so you recruit others and sit back as if it's okay to cause bloodshed over a flag with the true tourist, betrayed by your government itself. You are the MONSTER behind the show. I can't see your face, but I hear the voice of your plans. I'm not moved awake as if night skip my house without a kiss to say good bye. God you're the only way please have mercy on us as we travel through the journey of life, protect us of the unseen, send your angel Saint Michael to battle for our soul. Mental health is at risk, who can we trust when everything seems too good? Please keep our eyes open, out of the hands of our enemy. Amen. Prayer from a fallen saint forgive us, Lord, for we do not know what we are doing; thanks for loving me beyond any feeling I felt. My eyes could reach my arm, hold you forever like a dream dancing in the mind of pureness nothing bad like a child innocent eye blind from what the world truly is. Amen.

 *Eternity of Dreams*

THANKS FOR
LOVING ME

I f I could dream the dreams of you, that would be perfect for the eyes of your world; indeed, his opened, and there is nothing hidden. If I could breathe for you, dancing through your body, that will be amazing to have a part of us in sync with the season. The sunset is worth millions, there are no minds like ours set aside for you and me. The star sits in the skies so peaceful without noise, just the way you like it. I wouldn't want to change it. It's a part of you. I think you are unique, amazing, and special, like you were made for me, placed on the planet earth for me. I have never felt so complete. I call it déjà vu; thanks for allowing me to be a part of your existence. Please don't change the magic made above the star; I was there as a foundation to hold you until the last breath I take. It's you always, and I'll visit you in and out of dreams night or day. Nothing can keep us apart. The air you breathe. The wind that holds you is my love is a gift to you. I

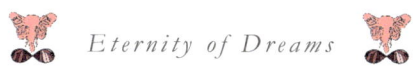

promised the first day I saw you, and I'll never let you go, growing as tall as the oak tree with you. Thanks for loving me.

April 13, 2018

I AM CLOSED
TO YOU

I'm not sure why you're in my house, you're not welcomed. I know how ignorant you can be; I chose not to deal with it. I'm happy to meet the night pretending to sleep just to ignore your voice, hoping you go away; you're filled with negativity, and my eyes can't reach you. The door of my world has been closed. I don't care for it at all. It seems like a nightmare walking in dreams of days. The way you speak to me in a disrespectful manner, I am confidently looking eye to eye with you, your soul is sick and twisted. I wonder why things happen to you. You have none of your nine children. I'm done. Let me out anyway; I just want to be as far as I can, the time wasted with your lie; you are a horrible person, motherless boys filled with rage hidden behind the flower. Give anything you can to when it's time for the show, and the monster will appear, the illusion of what a guy, but looking for a mother to fix. It is not a woman's

job to break a girl, to control her with drugs and sex; you are beyond sex, and you are more of a lifeless body with emotion. As the days go by, I grow more and more away from you. In a way, it causes trauma to my brain; I can't recall or recognize the scent at all. Without traces to follow, a love that never exists, just built on false illusion. The gift seems fake to the boy. I thought I could fix it. It drives me crazy at the same time, I'm closed to you.

April 4, 2018

THE LOVE OF MY SOUL

I went on my visit today blessed, and towards the end, I almost lost my breath returning my children.

It was foreign to me every time. When you leave me. I'm empty and lost; a piece of me goes with you Mom; so sorry, please forgive me. I'll make sure we will never be a part of the money-making business. The evil plot off having children like a business, this mom has a different focus, willing to fight for mine? I'm different from others, and I am a rare flower growing, don't need much; I can still grow in any season with or without the sun. I believe in myself. I believe in my children, they are warriors, and they are untouched just like me. As long as they can hear my voice or see me, it gives my babies hope. I haven't gone anywhere waiting for you, the love of my soul.

March 7

LOST MYSELF IN YOUR WORLD

I lost myself in your world like a hug from the ocean. Catching my breath is what I do best. The calls I call on Christmas, she answers my heart. I never knew how much I loved you, but at the same time, you never desired me, and I am to blame for your actions. I agree he accuses me of cheating. I would go back in my mind and question myself; could it be true? Have I been honest and true to you? The mental disorder of paranoia gets the best of me; I can't stop crying. It hurts so bad, reopening my broken heart. I'm falling to my knees crawling, asking 'Why you can't be the man of my dreams?' 'Why are you?' When I feel my heart flutter, I'm praying to the Lord to give me the strength to move on from it. I have spent so many painful memories questioning myself if I am beyond the star for you. 'Am I special enough to shine like the sun in any area of his life? Is it enough that I chase you through dreams just for me to be

whole, knowing you were poison to me?' I have given up everything and lost myself in your world.

12/25/2017

EVIL BLACK

He is a married man who think he desires to be with other women to sleep with at night. When he kissed his wife, he has already kissed everyone. She had a man who blessed her with two beautiful babies a family man who gave her the world, she traded him in for some tail. She keeps calling him with no answer, he's married now. She running after him, he don't want no family with you, you just feel different that's it. He can't even be there for his family. What makes you different? Your hair colors? He was flirting with me to enter my gate. He tells me how much money he has. I'm not moved at all. He tries with another girl going through a break-up, and you prey on her emotions. She smiles, dates a married man like it's the right thing to do. She doesn't see her value. When I see him, my soul turns to tell me that you are not a man in my eyesight, you're just a boy. Why ignore your value? Why give her lies on her wedding day? You are evil black.

12/3/2017

BACKBONE

He never had a BACKBONE at all, like a helpless puppy. She could never take my place as a mother. She just moved from her mom's house. All of the sudden, you grow a backbone overnight. She has you feeling like a new person. She doesn't know who you truly are. We started off just like that; I promise you will not even get close to touch my world when you start having your own with this straight dog hair children without grace. I wouldn't just lay down and allow you to come and get mine; you're out of your mind, you never had a dream, would never reach you, and give you a kiss of rest. The actions you have caused, the pain you have caused for my children and me, you are pure evil. I forgive you. The Lord forgives you, for you know not what you do.

11/6/2017

TOGETHER SOON

When I see a picture of you I catch my breath as the tear falls, mommy loves you. No matter what, I'll never leave you. I'm just away for a moment. I'm not far. I dedicated my days to you. Please know I'm still yours truly. I never thought a mistake could hurt so much, like an open wound. I never intended to cause any pain. I know that in the morning, you both will wake up looking for me, because I look for you too. I'm sorry for everything. My house is so lost without a foundation. It's both of you. Mommy loves you always. We will be together soon.

August 4, 2017

DIFFERENT VIEW

If I was raped and got pregnant, no one could have told me anything, not even religious, and it's my body. I choose this life. I might go through trauma. There is a rainbow in the midst of things. My baby will help me heal no matter where it comes from. It's still my child. I love you the same as if you were made from a special place without love. My true healing begins the moment you are born and let us face the world together. I'll pray each day for God's grace to give me the strength to go through it. I wouldn't have thought twice of going to the doctor to get rid of you. You're a part of me. I'm a part of you. My one true blessing was you, my baby. Even though I lost myself, even my life against my will, I still love you. The devil won't have his hands in my plans... Excuse me if my view, while away in my living room of imagination, no judgments here; the moment I found out I was pregnant, I found love with you before my eyes meet yours. May the angel of grace guide the unborn babies that didn't make it who were ordained to change the world against all

odds. I love you all. I chose life in memory of you. We can both be different, never fit in as if Mom and Daddy had wonderful plans for you in a perfect made circle. The truth is you just need to know that mom just needs you. That's fine, it doesn't matter what society has made up as a family. I was made to carry you in my womb for nine months. God gave me strength and comforted me as I brought this amazing baby to this world; that is all that matters. I love all the future babies that weren't blessed to see the morning smile, the night chase the stars across the skies, or hearing mom's voice, touch, and scent just because she is mine. Mother, I love you. Always a different view.

April 4, 2017

ONE MORE TIME

I need you to be like medicine to a blood heart's memories, from being a flat line. I'm going through the day without you. It's the most difficult time of the season being empty inside, you're the only one to complete me. I had a couple in the past, but it's the way you move my soul that gets me to stick. He moves on with his life. I become a breeze that passes by. I wonder if you ever dream of me and see what we could have become. The eyes of the universe, I see it in you. The heart of the ocean, I can rest within your waves, getting lost in the hallway of your soul. While tossing like the tides when you're near me. I miss the days of being yours truly. Just for a moment, laughter will fill my cup, and it will overflow like a river of the unknown. The way night looks like when I'm dreaming of you, and we fit so well like puzzle pieces. The chapter has ended on this magical road. If I could be yours truly one more time.

12/23/2015

I PROMISE

I have become humble over the years. My attitude was nasty, and the world did not accept me. The hand of the clock couldn't tell me anything, I was in a world of my own, but when night comes, I will pour my heart out until it runs dry. I pray and close my eyes. Lord, if this step I take, would you take the next for me? The Lord has given me morning and night, and His promise could never fade away. I always wonder how it would be to have a mother, you were supposed to be mine, and she takes you away from me the coldest feeling, and summer is just beginning... I love you before I ever knew you were my grandma. I always wanted to have a mother, and it was you, when the tears would fill my eyes, you would catch me, and you wouldn't be that far behind. I don't care what people say about you, you will always be mine, and I'll be yours until time stops, and beyond the stars, it could never end. I think of my brother and sister and how they're still trying to understand why mama never cared. I thought love would drive bad things away... My

prayer is, please don't let them get lost in the street. Give them peace... If they need something, Lord, just hold them. I wish I could help you, but I'm lost myself, no matter how far apart we are, I love you always, and stay above water. It will get better, I promise...

9/26/2015

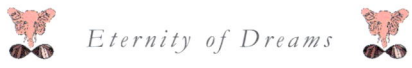

JUST YOU

Your eyes are like magic; the smile you have has become a key, opening up the gate of my soul. When you are in my mind, I feel so light weight. My body feels like a cloud floating in your perfect world. The mystery of you, to get to see you working, and there is no touching but just imagination going wild as our eyes connect like a show beyond space. My favorite place to be at, even though we are not a couple, just being friends is fine with me. What a wonderful high I get after you pass by me and ask about my day, what a special day just with your thoughts. Just you.

Dominique 9-1-2015

SOMETHING ABOUT LAST NIGHT

He told me after school that he'll bring dinner and a movie in just a second. It felt so real, but I knew it was just false hope. I'm waiting for you while holding the hand of summer, while dancing in winter. If I let go, would you take my hand to keep me from falling? I close my eyes and stay in summer where I know you never left me. Who do you think I am? Your journal book, you cannot poison my pages with all your lies, or do I tickle you and make you laugh? My feelings are not a toy to be played with. I am human just like you, remember you were the one who walked away from me. I never cheated on you. Now you want to waste my time, how about having dinner with yourself and finding out why you're such a horrible person? Find yourself before you get into another relationship. Something about last night.

3/19/2014

EXPO LINE

I have seen a young man with a little girl that sat right across from me, which made my heart drop. I said, 'What a wonderful thing of a parent, that makes you a wonderful person, where nothing even matters anymore except this little one called future'. Not only have I changed my whole world for you, because there was no other way of living except for you. The person I was years ago could not even imagine being a parent and caring for another life. The lord has given me the best gift the day that I found out I was a mother. I promise no matter what happens, mom will always be with you through the last song of time. I will never stop loving you and being your mother.

2/3/2014

WE GROW A PART

He told me we were growing apart, so I fade away, but he didn't know I had his heart from the beginning. He sent a message to me saying he misses me. He was stuck on me like a number on a clock, but it's too late. Remember, we grow apart. I love you beyond the length of the skies, the closeness of the stars. My world was you, and your soul was home away from home, a vacation from this crazy world, you were my fun place; days were endless, time was unspoken. I would think of words to say when I have seen you; he never pays attention to his words, but a new look on him lost within the ocean, hand dreams toss just because we grow apart, but you will never know how I truly love you, and when you said we grew apart my world was gone. My eyes poured out like a waterfall, so sad and blue. I had to keep in mind you said we have grown apart...

1/6/13

MOTHER

When we were in placement, we cried out for you in a dream, but you didn't hear us. Mom had a disease that has more power over her, but we loved you thinking it could cure you of your sickness. I want to fill the whole of your soul to feed you where you didn't hunger for the drugs. I want you to be there for the baby, but years have passed, and we have grown. I remember how close we were like paper and paint, but now we are so far apart, we are like strangers. The only thing we are bounded by is blood. I see myself in the kids like a mirror that brings a tear to my eyes. I was a little girl who wanted mommy, but she was too busy for me. We faded away, so did you. I don't understand how you can find rest at night knowing my siblings may be sleeping on the street. Mom, you created this pain where it hold us like hands and shake us. I remember you saying they're grown, and it's not my responsibility, but you brought us into this world. How can we move forward, knowing mom didn't love us enough to keep us

together? I don't care if we're miles away. Remember, I love you always from my soul. Be strong.

1/6/2014

DEAR MOM

I fell asleep thinking of you, and it was the sweetest thing ever. As I woke up the next morning, the air was full of your scent. The breath of heaven fills my lungs, your wings fluffy white with purple at the tops, loyal and true. She holds me like a child. I love you, grandma, always and for eternity... Oh mom, how I missed your smile, and the days were so endlessly full of happiness. The time we spent together was priceless, like a pearl so fine and one of a kind. I believe the Lord called you home because you were too good for the world; there were not enough hands to hold such remarkable women like yourself... You will always be my mom, no matter what. When my tears fell, you caught them. When I was alone in this world without direction, the love you had for me kept me from falling and also becoming lost in the hands of sadness. I would like to thank you Lord, for blessing her in my life, even if it was a short time, Dear mom.

10/29/2013

MY SWEET MONROE

Oh! Monroe, how I love you with my whole heart. When I look into your eyes, the tears are there, and pain breaks my heart. I wish I was there to stop it and protect you. See everything, and they will pay forever. You cried. The hands of dreams will wrap around their necks like vines and will never let them go. The wind can't reach your lungs and breathe for you, may you think of me in your last thoughts I miss you Monroe, it depends on you, the time on a clock dances every hour, and the days are made specially for you. Please don't be sad. Take it one day at a time. To My Sweet Monroe.

10/24/20

SUMMER TIME

She was my world and a mother. When I had a question, she was my answer. I wake up this morning, and the cold air dances around my body and my breath was as if you never left my side. I could feel your wings and even closer the air that you breathe. I had never imagined life without you could be such a lonely place... I'm writing a poem to say I love you with my soul and my heart always. She was my star, beyond the universe... I will tell them how great you were. I could search in the clouds and get lost in spaces as long as I know you will be my next step. What a beautiful life to share with my best friend, mother, and everything. I pray that you continue to watch over us... Angel of winter, but her voices are like summer time.

I just thought of you and with one sweet taste, my mind is blown, dancing as if I just escaped from the earth just to be with you. My favorite drugs that keep me going with no worries of coming down the roller coaster. Just get me by until night, until I'm feeling numb. I can't feel anything, the phone rings; it was

grief and I couldn't take the call. Her voice was on my voicemail, it is like the ocean was crashing against my soul. I am not ready to let you go for eternity. I will escape with you in this world of magic, spill out like a waterfall. I never knew I loved you this much, even in your passing. I just want you. This hit that I take with your name on it, the smoke that makes love throughout my body. This energy, please feel it beyond a physical form. It is your spirit that has me wrapped like winter hidden among the green hills where the angel flies above. This drug is so different. I wake up with the taste of you just to get by; everything goes numb. I never met a person like you that brings endless hugs from dreams to daydreams and with my soul you will remain. The beat of my heart is with you, every beat lets me breathe for you, lets me bring your gift to the world, lets me share this amazing journey. I am so blessed to be able to be in your present, and I love you for eternity. You can always find rest within me. I will keep knocking because I know you will always answer pure, loyal, and true.

SLEEPING ANGEL

This is a story of a sleeping angel with many stories that tell how magical you were; the sun will follow you like a shadow within the streets; hidden within you and all are welcomed to go. It's a puzzle when I see you, I became lost feathers from your wings. He left behind his tears that pour into the street and call it home, a hidden place where no one knows anything about him, just the feeling of loving his smiles, hugs, and also thoughtfulness. A woman can bring you paradise and on the same path, make you feel alone and lost in the summertime, hidden slight pain, smiling through tears, even though I am broken no one sees it. I am beyond repair. Just a simple friend who knows me would make it worthwhile. Thanks for sharing your story with me. My favorite part of the story was you. If I had known, I would have carried you like the leaves on a tree. My dreams will welcome you with loving arms, my sleeping angel.

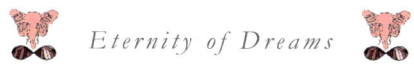

Made in the USA
Monee, IL
10 June 2026

52191942R00036